T0090477

RESIGNED TO SUCCESS

"Using an Exit Plan to Build Hope,
Energy, and Success in a Business"

SCOTT WHITE AND LARRY LINNE

authorHOUSE®

AuthorHouse™
1663 Liberty Drive
Bloomington, IN 47403
www.authorhouse.com
Phone: 833-262-8899

Published by AuthorHouse 03/27/2023

ISBN: 979-8-8230-0420-6 (sc)
ISBN: 979-8-8230-0419-0 (e)

Print information available on the last page.

CONTENTS

INTRODUCTION BY SCOTT WHITE

I decided to write this book to share my personal exit from my business journey, but more importantly, I wanted to share the critical components that made my journey successful and rewarding.

Unfortunately, I have witnessed numerous people get perpetuation wrong. Most of them had the best intentions in mind while going through their journey. Others were just focused on themselves, getting the best deal for themselves, despite their business, their team, their community, and other key stakeholders—and yes, in some cases at the expense of their families.

Too many people don't give this event the priority it deserves. They're not honest with themselves. They're not transparent and collaborative with the key stakeholders who will be impacted by their decision.

As you will read throughout the book, time is the number one asset you can have in planning your exit. Not giving yourself enough time will cause poor planning, choosing the wrong successor(s), and not being prepared personally for the next step for yourself, your family, and your team. Way too many people don't value the time element of the human side of succession planning.

People work decades growing their businesses. Then when the time comes to make one of the biggest decisions of their life, they fail. Some of them spend more time planning their next vacation than their exit event.

I clearly didn't want this to happen to me, my business, and my family. Proper perpetuation and business continuity was so important to me that I wanted to make this last journey with my business as special as any I ever experienced.

Getting this right is one of the most rewarding events of my career—and possibly of my life achievements.

Making sure I didn't do this alone was also critical to my journey's success. I decided to engage Larry Linne CExP™ to guide me through the journey. I have great respect for Larry's experience, knowledge, and unique ability to navigate the financial and human side of exiting a business. Those elements are clearly important, but it was even clearer that he cares about me personally, my family, and my business. He wanted me to be successful. From his commitment to keeping me focused from the very first challenge of "writing" My Resignation Letter™ to building the plan, executing it at the highest level never wavered. He challenged me consistently throughout my journey. I am thrilled that Larry decided to be a part of the writing of this book as he is helping me capture the reality of what happened, and I know he will bring value to those reading about my experience.

I am very proud of my exit as the result has proven to be incredibly successful. The experience was a joy to work through and has created wealth, opportunity, and joy to the lives of many people I love and appreciate. I hope this book will help give you a road map to finding how, why, who, and what will be most important to you on your journey.

Resigned to Success will guide you through why most

firms fail, the importance of getting started on the journey, the need for long-term planning with contingencies, how hope created the energy for performance and success, managing the timing of the final exit, and ultimately how to leave an organization in better shape than when it was given to you.

I experienced incredible guidance from Larry Linne through my journey and felt I would give the reader a gift by asking Larry to recap each chapter with his advice on the topic. You will see why he was such a powerful resource as you read these "Larry's Insights."

CHAPTER 1

MOST FIRMS FAIL

We started the journey with Larry spending a lot of time educating me on the realities of the failures of perpetuation. We don't typically hear about the failures because people justify the outcomes they receive in perpetuation and only talk about the positives.

It's like listening to someone talk about that one big win they had in a stock investment. They talk about the massive run-up of a stock and how it was such an amazing winner. But they don't tell you about all the loser stocks and investments they have made in their life.

The stories you hear of millions of dollars of wealth transfer, ESOP models that make employees owners, and internal and external transfers of ownership typically sound great. Unfortunately, the untold stories of how much money was left on the table, large value decreases, valuations accepted below the financial needs of the seller, ESOP failures, and cultures destroyed are more often the reality. I have had late-evening discussions with numerous past business owners who, after a few beers, will tell the real story of how disappointed they were in the final transfer choices they made. Most people came to the conclusion that they had no other option.

That is a sad narrative that should never be said by a business owner. When you own the business, you have all the choices. With only a few exceptions, if you plan far enough in advance and make the right decisions, you can accomplish all your objectives and goals.

One business owner who sold his business to a private equity company said, "I thought this was going to be great. After a few months of honeymoon transition, I realized I had lost more control than I expected. Coming to work is no fun now, but at least I have a huge check and will be getting more as we continue in our relationship."

Again, this is a sad outcome that didn't have to happen.

The simple reality is that people fail in perpetuation because they don't plan, don't plan for all the necessary components, or don't follow through and execute on the plans they do.

Failure comes in many forms in perpetuation.

- Not accomplishing the core desired purpose of the business. This purpose could be transferring ownership to family, staying independent, receiving the highest financial return possible, or numerous other potential goals.
- People not ready to take on leadership roles in the proper time.
- Poor financial performance during the run-up period of perpetuation (not enough free cash flow/growth to justify the sale).
- Not having unplanned strategies in place (death, disability, family issues, key employees leaving, etc.).
- No willing or capable buyers (internally).
- Seller really doesn't want to sell and holds on too long, thus eliminating potential options.

- Lack of personal financial planning to be able to sell the business.
- No clarity of what the current owners will go to or leave when they exit.
- Lack of inspiration to future leaders to prepare themselves for transition. Usually due to prior owners stating things like "Just let me know when it is time to go."
- Not understanding the financial models that exist with numerous methods of selling the business.
- Overall lack of financial acumen and being taken advantage of in a sale.
- Current or future partners not aligned and cohesive.
- Using CPAs, attorneys, and advisors who are not well versed in exit strategy or don't have knowledge of your industry and options available. They may not understand the complete picture and advise you in silos of their expertise.

These problems exist because business owners don't spend time learning the complexity of proper exit planning, don't follow through to complete the necessary planning, and don't stay the course while executing and modifying the plan as things change. In the end, every one of the items listed above can, and probably will, reduce the financial rewards and eliminate desired options for a successful transition.

I am proud to say we avoided and fought through the items above and made it to the desired finish line.

SCOTT WHITE AND LARRY LINNE

Larry's Chapter 1 Insights

- Planning and execution are lacking and damaging potential value for business owners.
  - o Less than 30 percent of entrepreneurial companies I have engaged have clear plans in place for perpetuation.
  - o Less than 5 percent of entrepreneurial companies I have engaged have complete plans in place that include financial perpetuation and business continuity and are actively executing those plans.
- Failure is hidden. The world accepts mediocracy way too often. It is easy to brag about a $4 million sale of your business. It is unfortunate that it could have been twice that number and not left with a damaged culture whereby half of the people will leave the company in the next two to three years. A business owner will typically far exceed all goals if they plan and are disciplined to execution.
- Leaving a business is hard for many business owners because the business and the role define them. This is a huge influence toward poor decisions in perpetuation strategy and execution. It is critical for an exiting owner to have something to go to so they don't constantly fight leaving something.
- As we shared previews of this book, I received the same feedback I have received for many years in guiding people through perpetuation. They have stated this topic creates anxiety, depression, and major battles. People have thrown documents,

hidden paperwork in closets, and trashed the book only to come back again and ask for another copy. Please know this book will trigger emotions and that is OK. Push through, and it will be worth it.

CHAPTER 2

THE JOURNEY TO MY RESIGNATION LETTER

My journey of perpetuation began with my first opportunity to purchase into the company as a minority partner in 1993. In 1998 I had the opportunity to purchase as an equal partner with two others. My new partner Chris and I became partners with Bill, who was one of the previous shareholders who remained, and the three of us became the managing partners.

This transition was terrible! We had no training or education on owning and running a business. We were equal partners and just took on the roles we thought necessary to get the job done. We look back and realize we were incredibly lucky to have survived.

We were small and had to manage cash flow to stay afloat. We worked together and did whatever it took to grow and make the business successful. In retrospect, I believe this was partly successful because we were small and could see all the moving parts and were able to execute with speed. I am confident a larger firm could never accomplish what we did as a small business.

I realized how difficult it was to run the business by winging it with no training or experience very soon after taking things over. I vowed to not repeat that with my future partners.

When we did our next perpetuation event in 2011, our third partner sold his shares of the business to three young salespeople. We had the CEO and COO/CFO positions nailed down with Chris and me. However, we were growing fast and would require additional leadership roles with these new partners, even if it was informal leadership.

We began our first good move in effective business perpetuation. We put the three new partners into formal ownership training before they became owners. They went to training with Larry's company for two years before becoming owners. This included financial training, leadership, operations (core understanding), strategic thinking, decision-making skills, and more. We wanted high ownership acumen in our partners and wanted to make certain they understood the responsibility that comes with owning a business.

When they became owners, they had roles within the organization as leaders. This included department leadership, product line development leadership, strategic planning and execution responsibilities, and the general responsibility to be leaders of people.

They did a nice job and made a positive impact on the business. A few years later, we realized none of them had the desire or the aptitude to take over the CEO, CFO, or COO roles of the organization as we became a larger company. They were all incredibly talented in sales roles as well as core product leadership, but running the company the size we were becoming was going to be a very different job from what I was doing at that time. I didn't feel confident we were on track to have the leadership required to run a future $30 million agency.

To accomplish our desired long-term perpetuation desires, we realized we had to get specific about our goals and make certain all stakeholders needs were met. Therefore, we decided to get clear about our goals for all stakeholders. We realized we wanted to take great care of our clients because they were our lifeblood. We believe all perpetuations should create a better client experience. We also realized we needed to continue to grow our client base, no matter what we did with our company strategies. This growth would allow the financial means to accomplish whatever we would decide as a perpetuation path. Another goal was to maintain a lifestyle as owners where we had control of our local decisions. We also wanted to continue to create value for our current shareholders and have a perpetual opportunity for future people to become partners and create personal wealth.

Soon after establishing the clarity of our goals, we found a financial model and partner that would allow us to do a financial transaction to help us continue to run our business and not worry about who would eventually write us checks for our ownership. (More on this in the appendix.) We found a capital partner that would enhance our ability to serve our employees and clients at a high level. It also provided the financial rewards to our current and future partners. This was a tremendous step in helping us continue our goals as owners of a business. We continued having ownership, and our future employees would have opportunities for ownership wealth creation.

Our prior planning and execution put us in a solid

place to capture this opportunity. Having great growth, development of people, and a very high profit margin gave us a great positioning with this new capital partner. We were fortunate to take the financial piece off the table and now just focus on the real difficult part: the business continuity.

As we thought about the business continuity that continued to face us, Larry made the comment that we didn't need to replace ourselves; we needed to find someone who could run a company two to three times larger than we were that day. We needed someone better than us! The company was roughly fifty people and $10 million in revenue. He suggested we need someone with the skills to run a $20 million to $25 million company if we wanted to be successful in growing the business.

We had a long-term strategic vision of being $30 million by 2030. Larry was right. We needed people who would have the skills to run a $30 million agency!

This was not just an issue and objective for me as CEO. Chris was the CFO/COO and would be departing before I would, and we realized we would need four people to take on the responsibilities of our two jobs.

We needed a CFO and a COO to replace Chris's roles. I needed a CEO and a sales leader to replace my two roles.

At that point, we had to develop a plan for perpetuation of our roles. We had reached a place in our journey that we had to accomplish a lot in less than five years if we were going to be successful.

It seemed insane that we would need more than twelve years from the start of our journey to make certain we accomplished all our stakeholder objectives. It took time to plan, develop, manage contingencies and roadblocks, and execute.

But now we were at a place where we had clarity of the need to transition key positions and find the talent to bring successful business continuity to our firm. If we didn't, we would most likely fold into another company within our parent organization or simply fade as a business and be a very bad investment for our new partner.

Larry's Chapter 2 Insights

1. Time is the enemy of financial perpetuation and business continuity. It is rare for a company to get it all right. Companies will compromise financial rewards, people commitments, personal goals, and goals of others in the organization due to not having time to execute.

2. Time and purpose must be aligned. Being purposeful in development as well as recognizing truths of the future growth and aging of people will allow for a chance to meet all the goals.

3. Being clear of all stakeholder objectives is also important. If you don't have clarity of these objectives, it will be easy to compromise what is really desired.

4. Once a plan is developed, having the time to execute is critical. It will most likely take longer than you think. Create buffers to execute.

CHAPTER 3

LARRY'S RESIGNATION LETTER

When Larry told us to build a business continuity plan, I thought it would be an easy one- to two-hour session to lay it all out. It ended up taking us over two years of continued work before we were able to have the plan in perfect condition.

We took a first run at building this plan in 2015 but didn't have complete clarity of how it would work until 2017. The plan included every key leadership position, including CEO, CFO, COO, sales leader, key department heads, salespeople, and estimating new positions based on growth.

We had to determine estimated departure dates, potential new hire dates, start dates of training and development if the candidates were internal, compensation impact, and contingencies.

This was daunting because of the uncertainty of the future but really became a challenge when we started challenging people as to their estimated exits. It was painful to watch many of us hesitate on giving exit dates. We didn't want to put anything on paper and were not ready to give clarity of our departures.

This was another spot where Larry had to eventually step in. In 2017 Larry told us he wrote his resignation letter to his partners in his company. He said he wrote a letter that spelled out how great the people were, how they had focused on key replacement skills and developed those skills to be greater than his, and how the company had done everything necessary to grow profit to be able to pay for his exit. The letter also laid out how every stakeholder was in a great place, and it was time for his departure.

I was shocked when he told me about and read the letter. I couldn't see him leaving his business at that time. He was still in his fifties and I had no idea he was ready to go.

Then he hit me with the punchline. The letter was post dated seven years!

Larry had sent a message to his team about what it would take for him to leave the business and allow them to take over.

He told me the story of another firm he was coaching at the time. He said the CEO had no idea when he would leave the business. He had a few very talented people in the organization that could become the future leaders of the business. Unfortunately, he would tell them what many business owners tell stakeholders, "When it is time for me to go, please promise me you will tell me."

He also said the leader wouldn't provide leadership training or development to the next generation of leaders because it may make them feel entitled to his position. The next-generation leaders became complacent, disengaged, and just *did their job*. They had no hope of getting key leadership positions because they believed the CEO would have to die in his work chair before they could have an opportunity.

The lack of hope and, to some extent, the depression of some of the top talent at this firm was hard to watch.

So much potential could have been unleashed but instead just went through the motions.

After Larry delivered his letter to his team, he believed telling his team about the opportunity and timing would give them energy and drive to do great things. He was right! His team jumped on the items in the letter and started developing skills to replace him.

The results were amazing. People were developing faster than any time in the company's history, revenue was growing, profit increased, and the hope and energy for the organization were electric!

Larry said, "I believe when people have clarity combined with hope and opportunity, they will strive to thrive."

I have watched his team the last few years after this letter was written and it has been amazing to watch the focus on development. His team initially took on areas where they were interested. After a couple of years of development, Larry became more specific in leading his team into the future. He continued to break down areas that had not been captured by future leaders and was partnering with individuals on areas that had to be strong before he could leave. They are digging deep into replaced skills as well as skills and talents that had to be in place for future growth.

Larry's experience intrigued me, but it also terrified me. What if I don't want to leave at that date? What if we aren't ready? What if I don't have complete clarity of what I am going to do next in my life? How can I say things that won't be true? I realized every business plan we had ever put together was a guess. I knew we could adjust a plan, but it was so valuable to work toward something specific. The head trash of not planning was selfish and didn't have a valid justification.

It was clearly time for me to write my resignation letter.

Larry's Chapter 3 Insights

- My Resignation Letter™ was one of the luckiest strategies I have implemented in my career. I was motivated by a couple of executives who refused to be purposeful in the development of next-generation talent. This was especially true when I realized they were fighting against personal fear of becoming less valuable to the organization.

- I have convinced some executives to write the letter even if they don't share it with their teams. Getting it on paper starts the process and can help a CEO see the path to success.

- Plans are always more effective than just hoping it all works out.

- The letter should be an exciting read. It should tell a story of an amazing future with details about financial success, human development, client experience excellence, and even industry disruption and innovation.

- Write the letter, get the team engaged, discuss it often, and adjust actions on a regular basis to make the letter a reality.

CHAPTER 4

MY RESIGNATION LETTER™

Larry and I had discussed the fact that eventually I was going to retire from the agency. He had shared several other business owners' stories he had worked with over the years that did it well and unfortunately a number that didn't do it so well. As always in life, we can learn as much from people who do things well as from those who didn't. His challenge was very clear. You are going to retire someday from your business. Why not do it the best way possible? Why not control the event and the message? If you don't, others will do that for you, and it usually doesn't work to your advantage.

I am a big fan of Barry Sanders, who was an elite running back for the Detroit Lions. Barry was on his way to becoming the greatest running back in NFL history. To accomplish that, it would require him to stay in the league long past what any human body should endure. The ego of most humans who would have that opportunity would drive them to throw caution to the wind and play until they couldn't walk again.

Barry Sanders abruptly retired and walked away from the NFL in his prime! He shocked the entire NFL by leaving when he still had a lot of gas in his tank.

Our partner Bill did a Barry Sanders departure, and it was impressive. We weren't ready for him to leave us personally, but he did an amazing job of preparing us for his professional departure.

I was always so impressed with Barry's departure. I have seen so many athletes and business executives stay well past their prime. In many cases, it is sad to watch them deteriorate and perform at lower levels as they try to hang on to the glory.

I knew that I didn't want to be "that guy" who hung on too long and was going to be a Barry Sanders who left my career sitting on top. My work was not going to define me as a human, and leaving while on top was a way to prove it. I always said I would prefer to have them pulling on my collar to keep me around rather than pushing me out the door with two hands to my shoulders.

When Larry shared with me what others had done and we began the journey of "owning" my exit strategy, we called it the "Barry Sanders model."

It was now time to write My Resignation Letter™.

Larry was very clear that this initial letter was a starting point. It would be the first draft of what potentially would lead to a few more as I gained more clarity of my exit plan. It would be the first step of my journey.

It was now approximately two years since Larry had first addressed business continuity and how I needed to write my letter. When he first told me of the process, I was intrigued about what he was sharing with me, but I wasn't ready. Now that we were discussing my exiting the business more regularly in our monthly coaching calls, he was setting the stage with me on how to consider doing this. It also helped to know that he is a few years younger than I am and he was beginning to look out three to five years as well on his exit strategy but had already written his letter. We had other examples to mold my strategy as well as Larry getting serious about how this process might ultimately shape his future exit.

Back to that challenge to write that first draft of my retirement letter. We are in early 2019 now. My timeline is beginning to take shape, at least in my head and in our coaching calls. I committed to him that I would take on his challenge and write my first draft. It wasn't unusual during our monthly calls that I agreed to do something he challenges me to do, but instead of doing it right away, it might take me months. OK. He might even suggest longer in some things. But as I know he would agree, when I commit to him that I will do something, I do it, just not maybe as soon as he expects.

Now I am actively thinking that I am going to write this retirement letter. I mean draft. I have all kinds of thoughts on how, where, and when I am going to do it. I knew I needed to write it, but my mind was racing all over the place. Was I doing this for Larry? Was I leaving too early? Was it really the right time? What if I did it wrong? What if I upset my partners? What if we picked the wrong successors?

Talk about head trash. I needed to create the right situation to be able to focus. I needed to get away and clear my head. I had used a concept of "on time" for years in my career. This was where I would go away from home and have zero distractions. It helps me get clarity and enough time to dive into something with no distractions. This was a big issue, and I had to get it right.

I needed to schedule the time away.

As a Michigan business owner who travels throughout the US, most people assume I live near Detroit. I do not. I live in the Upper Peninsula almost five hundred miles from Detroit. In my business, I regularly travel to and from the "lower peninsula." Most of the time is by car as air travel can be hit and miss in our rural area. Driving to Detroit, Lansing, or Grand Rapids, where most of my business took me, was a six- to eight-hour car ride each way. Most of my travel over the years was solo, which gave me a lot of time to think things through.

I had scheduled a trip to Lansing for some meetings, but I knew it would be a good time to think and develop my letter. My mind was as usual racing between multiple things. It was bouncing around between some personal and professional items. I distinctly remember that I was occupied with my commitment to Larry to get the initial draft done. In fact, I had a monthly call scheduled with him the upcoming week. I was able to focus on capturing some ideas of what could go into this letter. I dreaded the reality and finality of putting this to paper. I am not sure exactly why. Maybe because it would actually make my exit strategy become a reality. It might have been because it would be extremely hard to do. I had never done anything like this before.

However, on this day, for the very first time, I began to have clarity of what I wanted and needed to say in this letter. I finally had some energy to put pen to iPad. It was only going to be a draft, and no major commitments were being made, but it was a great and inspiring start.

As I merged on I-75 North from M-127 at Grayling, I had a strong urge to write down my thoughts before they disappeared. I needed to pull over somewhere. On I-75 North just south of Gaylord is a rest area around mile marker 252. It would be a good place to pull over and summarize my thoughts. I pulled into the rest area (seems ironic now that I look back) and stayed left in the truck parking section. I just needed to write my thoughts down quickly. I parked and grabbed my iPad from the passenger seat.

Fifteen minutes later, I had written my first draft of my retirement letter from my business. Yes, fifteen minutes. I honestly could not believe how quickly and easily it was to write it. I was not only surprised how fast and easily the words came to me, but it encompassed everything I wanted to letter to say. The other sensation I didn't expect to experience was how liberated I immediately felt by writing it and rereading it. I felt such a sense of relief. I was not prepared for this to be the day I would complete the letter, but it was done!

It took fifteen minutes and was easy to do. It was so liberating!

I first shared it with my wife, Jill, when I got home. She was actually very pleased with what she read. The following week, I shared with Larry in our monthly coaching call. He was pleased with it and grinned at how easy it was for me to write when I finally took the time to do it.

In September I shared with Chris and then with her and our new CFO, Rachel, in a joint session.

For the first time, my exit from my business was becoming real. My wife, my advisor, and my partners all now understood that this was going to happen.

As Larry had said multiple times, by writing this down, it is the beginning of the process. He couldn't be closer to the truth. My exit strategy journey was officially beginning. Shortly after this, I shared it with my adult children. In December I shared at our planning session with the other three partners and then to the team at our annual meeting in January 2020.

As I have reviewed and seemingly modified the original draft countless times, it amazes me that 90 percent was still the same as the original. The major changes were the dates. I established four dates that were all nine months apart. I was not 100 percent certain of my timing because there was a lot of work to do to identify my successor and coach and mentor him or her.

A key component that was clear to me was how much this was my journey. Larry had shared with me about others' journeys he had witnessed, but my journey would be unique. It was about me, my family, and my business. It had to be personal. There wasn't anybody else's that we could copy. Each of us has our own journey to follow. It is important to understand that and define what is important to you, your family, and your business.

We have already stated that we wanted this to be like a Barry Sanders model. I am no Barry Sanders, but I now had the chance to leave my job in my prime. I could move on to the next season of life and enjoy it!

There are a few other things Larry and I discussed that make sense for anyone to incorporate into an exit planning. As I said before, "Own it." Control the messaging. After all, it will define your "brand," so don't let others message it for you.

Build your communication strategy. Leave on your terms, but make sure both your family and your business are well positioned for your exit.

Lastly, as Larry and I always discussed, you need to not just be leaving your business but you must be going toward something else. Always striving for a bigger future. A healthy business succession planning strategy needs to position both the business and the departing owner for a bigger future.

Typically, the business is left in great hands with new and energized leadership, but you personally will have a long, healthy next phase of whatever you choose it to be.

I couldn't have been more pleased with how we addressed each of these over the next few years. Build *your plan,* share it with key stakeholders, and execute it better than anything that you have ever done before. Most importantly, utilize the number one planning asset of time! With time, all positive things are possible.

Larry's Chapter 4 Insights

- Scott really battled with the concept of writing his resignation letter. I find this to be true with most CEOs. They are terrified they will become irrelevant or create entitlement with the next generation. I have never found that to be reality. Everyone who has written a My Resignation Letter™ has had measurable improvements in the business and has found a rewarding exit from the business.

- Scott also did a great job of working through where he was going to go in the future. He didn't have perfect plans, but he had a great list of things he knew he would want to do and would enjoy. It is very hard to leave something but incredibly rewarding to go to something greater than our past. That opportunity awaits everyone!

CHAPTER 5

THE LETTER CREATED A SENSE OF URGENCY AND GREAT RESULTS

Now that the plan was clear in my mind and all the stakeholders saw a clear picture of hope for the future, it was time to get to work.

Chris VanAbel had been my partner from the beginning of our journey, and her successful transition was a huge priority for me as well. I care very much for her and her family. She impacted our business more than any individual over the past twenty-five years.

Chris and I would be leaving the business within a few months of each other. She had celebrated an incredible fifty years working at our agency. We needed to identify and mentor her COO and CFO roles and my CEO and sales leadership roles. It was extremely important that we got each of these decisions right. It was critical that we honor her legacy and not focus on me. We had co-led the success of this business and had been great partners along the way. We had been partners since 1998 and worked together since 1988. She has not only been my partner but will always be a cherished friend.

My letter was a moment of reality for her. We came into this business ownership together, and we realized it was time to allow others to take it to the future.

Chris had battled for many years about how she could

25

and would exit the business. She has worked with Larry and his team and struggled to get her arms around her perfect exit. I wanted to help her, but I knew she had to find her own way.

When my letter was final and presented, I believe it gave her the freedom and confidence to see the finish line more clearly. Don't get me wrong. Chris is and was fully capable of being her own person and making her own way. I just know that as we discussed my letter, she was clearly freer to talk about her exit and her plans.

After many years of struggling to plan her exit, she was more successful than I was from a speed standpoint. She managed to retire in less than nine months from the date she made the decision to leave. She also was a superstar in mentoring and training the CFO and COO. She left her roles in amazing shape and allowed me to feel confident in the work I was doing to transition my roles.

The resignation letter sparked a ton of energy from those taking the new roles. They knew clearly what had to be done to accomplish the transition and allow them to be the next leaders.

We exceeded sales plans, improved the sales leadership structure, built strong financial management systems, transitioned strategic and tactical planning roles, and even transitioned away from Larry Linne! Yes, our next-generation leaders connected with the next-generation leadership of Larry's company for future coaching.

Larry suggested the letter would initiate clarity and results. He was right! Our team realized how important it was to get everything right, and the sense of urgency and excitement drove above average results.

In 2013 we had identified a ten-year strategy of growing our agency revenue to $10 million, more than doubling our growth. Through all our succession planning and selling the business in 2015, we never wavered from our goals. In fact, we achieved our 2023 goal by the end of 2021! This was something that we all took great pride in.

Some examples of the energy that rose from the letter.

- The future CEO was a producer. He took on leadership training, built a national insurance program with other partners, and did it with a structure that would allow him to give the time to the future CEO role and drive growth through the program.
- The future COO/CFO joined a top-level executive development program, brought many of her learning into the organization, and improved our profit and productivity while training.
- Other salespeople jumped into leadership roles (unpaid) for personal growth and a show of commitment to future leadership.
- Next-generation leaders, on their own initiative, began meeting to discuss plans for exceeding growth goals, establishing a vivid vision for the future, and began execution prior to our exit.
- Third-party stakeholders began recognizing the strong leadership in our company. It gave them hope and we had specific examples of financial investment in our organization to reward the recognition of our powerful future.

- People were energized and excited about coming to work. Our effective employee turnover was zero. Our firm was beating industry norms for employee engagement, retention, and overall satisfaction.
- Our team was hitting industry leading growth results and EBITDA performance.

I have witnessed so many companies who slow down as leaders leave or retire in place. The loss of energy can cause major slowdowns to the business growth and in some cases permanent stagnation. Energy is contagious as is a major loss of energy.

I am so thankful Larry drove us toward the resignation letter and clarity of the future. Without it, I could easily see how we as leaders could have been solely responsible for the decline in our business. Instead, our backing off with clarity created an explosion in growth of revenue and profit and ultimately what I value: human development!

The concept of "less is more" really played out here. "Less" of us created a lot more for everyone else in the firm.

Larry's Chapter 5 Insights

- When people have clarity of what needs to be done to accomplish your exit, they will work hard to fill those roles. We experienced valuable personal development with most individuals and exceptional revenue and profit growth due to the hope, passion, and drive to attain certain skills.

- The entire process is a process to build hope and energy toward a target. Think of how your company can perform when everyone is striving to develop the skills of leading the firm.

- Not everyone will end up in a leadership role. But you and they will learn very early on if they have the grit and skills to reach the desired targets. If they don't, you will learn early and have time to find other talent.

- Scott did an amazing job of being inclusive in his approach to business continuity. Chris was a subject of every conversation, as were family, other partners, key employees, and many of the stakeholders. Keeping an eye on all stakeholders will make the journey special and more effective.

- I also want to recognize a common component of leaders exiting the business. Notice that both Scott and Chris required two people to replace each of their jobs. This is very normal for growth-based entrepreneurial companies. The leaders' jobs can turn into two to four jobs when they leave. Recognizing this reality will give you more confidence that the position can be transitioned.

- Today's business environment values and rewards energy more than time. What do you manage? Create energy in your organization and give time back to you and your people.

CHAPTER 6

MANAGING KEY STAKEHOLDERS

The multiyear plan became more complex as we dug into all the stakeholder needs. It would take time to understand and meet all the stakeholders needs and to make certain contingency plans were in place for any changes that may occur.

We later learned how important these contingency strategies were for the plan. Just know things will change!

The stakeholders were the owners of the firm, clients, employees, future leaders, and future owners and the families of all of these entities. We realized the number of lives we were going to impact and needed to get it right. Success would not happen with a last-minute decision and plan. We had to get started!

We wanted to own this and be proactive for the best interest of all parties. The legacy of any business will be clearly defined on how you leave. All of the stakeholders will be impacted with how we approached this. In our plan, we had to start with the recognition of every stakeholder that would be impacted and make sure we did our best to serve them all.

Our success was causing us continued problems. We were growing at a rapid pace and the internal perpetuation models were becoming even further out of reach.

In addition, all of the stakeholders would not only experience this transition intimately, but they will also have a significant impact on the plan's success. Perpetuation plans are not successfully executed in a secret room with the owner(s) of the business. Success comes from all stakeholders being aware and driving toward clear plans and goals.

The clarity of growth, financial performance, human development, client experience, and hard work it takes to execute are critical. If the company runs in the dark toward uncertainty, it will land in a place short of desired expectations. I learned in my discussions with Larry that the best time to plan for the exit in a business is the first day you start.

I knew this but continually put those plans off as it just didn't seem real to me for most of my early days in ownership. But when we realized the five people to one ratio in future owners to purchase current shares, I took my learning from Larry to heart and started working on that plan.

As mentioned earlier, we began with communication to future leaders and potential shareholders to make them aware of the sense of urgency and to get them prepared to do what they had to do for their success.

I can't express how critical communication is in this process. I have always believed in transparency and communicating realities to key stakeholders. People will not be able to perform if they do not know where you are going. As a leader, I have found that it is critical to over communicate to your team. You won't get complaints for overcommunication but will certainly be criticized for too little!

So we started to set the table that we (current senior

partners) wouldn't be here forever. One of the first exercises Chris Van Abel (partner/COO/CFO) and I (CEO and sales leader) did was, during one of our team meetings, abruptly get up and leave the room. We waited a few minutes then returned and shared with them that there would be a day in the future that we wouldn't be in the room with them. We also made it clear that there were two of us in our leadership roles currently, but when we were gone, there would be four people: a CEO, a COO, a sales leader, and a financial leader. We clearly didn't know who they were at that time. At that time, the whos weren't as important as the fact that in time we wouldn't be there. They needed to hear and see this to start to understand things were changing.

My family was also critical to the success of our plan. My wife was the very first person I shared the details of my future exit. I needed her not only to understand that very soon I was going to be *home for lunch!*

The obvious questions were asked.

- Why are we doing what we are doing?
- Are you ready?
- Are we ready?
- When do we have time to prepare?
- Can we afford it?
- Health insurance?
- Is everything going to change?
- What are we going to do?
- What will I do?

Being on the same page with her has been the most

important part of my plan. Nobody challenges me more than my wife (my best friend), and nobody has and will ever support me more than her.

I also have two daughters who needed to understand that Dad was going to be retiring. They both were excited for me but also expressed great concern if I was ready. How would Mom and I navigate a new phase together?

I had been in the business their entire lives so that was a big part of how they viewed their father. They not only asked thoughtful questions of me but also in confidence with Mom as well. Their feedback was very important to me, but as two very special adults, I wanted, needed, and valued their advice.

I had another important dynamic. Our partners have children working in the business. When you have family working with you in the business, it is important that they understand the transition of the business and your personal transition.

If they're part of your succession plan, it creates complexity that must be managed. My daughter was succeeding me as our sales leader. So we needed to be very thoughtful in getting this right for her, our team, and our family. I was fortunate that I was able to be there for two years to coach and mentor her.

This was another part of our success story. In each of the two years with one of my daughters in the role as our sales leader, our business set records for new business. The results surpassed anything we had ever accomplished with me at the helm! In fact I am reminded regularly that she is the "best sales leader" we have ever had!

Being transparent and vulnerable here. I was very

afraid of her failure. This fear was not because of her talent or abilities. The fear was how others would perceive and treat the CEO's daughter who had not been a successful salesperson in our industry, and my ego questioned, "Can anyone really do what I have been doing the past twenty years?" My transparency in saying this is necessary because I believe too many people fall into this trap. You can't let fear drive these decisions.

Getting outside advice was a key to success in this area. Larry figuratively punched me in the mouth with the idea. We were talking about business continuity and Larry suggested I move out of the sales leadership role and let my daughter take over. I knew she was capable, but I thought the organization would perceive she was being promoted just because she was my daughter. I didn't want that for her, for them, or me.

She was running the marketing and new business development for the company prior to this decision. I had to think a lot about this move because I didn't want her to fail or to have the firm go backward in our sales results. We needed the continued growth to justify our perpetuation strategies.

Larry asked me if she had the skill, potential, and drive to be successful in the position. I said she clearly did.

He asked me if I had built systems and structures that would allow for her to be successful. I responded that those systems were a big reason for our success. So yes, they were in place.

He asked me if I would be able to coach her for the two years through my transition and be a mentor to help her succeed? Again, I answered yes!

Larry said, "Make the move. She deserves it and you know she will be successful."

Of course, I was still concerned about perceptions. So I sought approval from my partners, and they agreed to make the move.

Getting it right with family in the business isn't easy. You must be very purposeful. Larry has guided me through this as he has worked with countless others who have had success and unfortunately way too many who didn't.

Once my daughter moved into the job, Larry directed us to helping to guarantee her success.

The first directive was that in her new role as sales leader that she needed to bring things to our COO and future CEO (who was still in sales but grooming to be CEO) before bringing them to me. This allowed the three of them to start to build trust among each other and solve things together without me getting involved.

Once again effectively "running the business" while I was still there. Countless times to her credit when our COO and incoming CEO met with me and updated me on things, they were surprised and pleased that she honored the chain of command and I had no idea what they were working on. That said, if they and or I believed it was important for me to get involved in any way, we would do so collaboratively as a team.

The second advice Larry challenged me with is once I exited the business, I would not be able to effectively give advice and counsel to not only my daughter but those other associates who I had been leading for decades. He shared that as a CEO I had intimate knowledge of the business and was able to give good advice. Once I was not in the business, I would quickly lose that perspective. At first, I didn't want to believe it, but then as I sat in meetings with the new leadership team, it became so clear that what they were planning and going to be executing would be rapidly evolving. I wouldn't know everything that I had known for decades within our business any longer. My instinct would be to help my daughter with every decision, but the right answer needed to always be "I would talk to your leadership team."

Most importantly, I would become Dad and hopefully she might want to share success and challenges with me without me asking her what's going on. During transition, I can watch and mentor her and the entire new leadership team. But as I transition to just being Dad, I will make it easy for her to get to know me in that new role and not think about the business.

Through all the fear and getting past my ego, it turned out to be incredibly successful. However, I want to be clear of why it was successful. I received good outside counsel, we had time to transition and mentor/coach, my partners were part of the decision, we provided good coaching and training for her, we planned out the transition details, and she is one talented young woman!

Larry's Chapter 6 Insights

- A proper exit should consider all stakeholders. This should include clients, prospects (market), employees, key employees, family, business partners, strategic partners, and yourself. You don't have to meet everyone's needs, but it is valuable to consider all the needs, prioritize them, and shoot for the greatest outcome possible.

- It is valuable to have third-party advice as you go through the process of determining skills and talents of those potentially replacing you. In this perpetuation, a few of the decisions were heavily questioned, and in a couple of cases, the partners were in complete disagreement on future hires. In the end, the decisions they made have already shown to be the best decisions and they are performing incredibly well. They had outside counsel in all of those decisions and the outside counsel helped them get past some biases and concerns.

- I find that many people want to control the company from the grave (not literally). They want to try to make every decision, so the future generation is guaranteed success. This isn't necessary. If you put the right people in place, they will make the right decisions in the future.

CHAPTER 7

IT'S A PEOPLE BUSINESS AND PEOPLE MAKE A GREAT EXIT FUN AND WORTH IT

It was during our planning session in December 2019. We finally all had clarity that I was going to exit the business in 2022. All key parties—family, partners, and identified future leaders—needed to have a voice at the table.

As stated earlier, in preparation for the 2011 succession event, we had identified three talented and valued associates that we wanted to be a part of the next event. They all became partners on April 1, 2011. I believed it was my responsibility as a leader to always be looking toward the future pertaining to our financial perpetuation. That most importantly included who would be leading and shepherding the business into the future. We had identified three young, talented individuals we wanted to have a seat at the table, along with one of the young partners from 2011, and we shared my resignation letter with the four of them. Once again, by being upfront and clear, it continued to allow us to move forward together.

Let me say how refreshing it is to be able to work through this journey with like-minded people who all had the same aligned interest. A great culture with great people not only can make this plan predictable and guaranteed but also a time to enjoy. I have looked forward to each phase of our plan because of the people I was working with and how we supported each other. The emotional support was one of the areas I had no idea I would need. This business had become to define who I was professionally for decades now. It had provided the lifestyle my family and I were so blessed to have.

I have had my times where in reflecting on what and how we have built this business I have become very emotional. I remember the first time it really hit me that this was really happening. I was going to leave "my business." It was March 2021. Like so many of us, COVID had impacted every facet of our lives. I had recently felt it was safe to travel once again. We, like so many businesses, were still operating virtually so I was encouraged by my wife to go to Florida, check on our condo, and work from there for a while. Not a hard decision as I live in the Upper Peninsula of Michigan on the "south beach" of Lake Superior, where we average two hundred inches of snow a year and winter usually lasts from late October to mid-May. We had left Florida in early March 2020 as the epidemic took over our lives. At that time, I had left my "three ring binder" at the condo as I was planning on returning in April to spend more time working on my plan.

As I sat alone in Florida on my patio overlooking the intercoastal waters, I was reading through all my plans. As I reviewed my "three ring binder" that had been sitting there for over a year and the work that we had continued to do the past thirteen months, it was a surreal moment in time.

First I reviewed my binder that had my first two drafts of my resignation letter along with correspondence from

Larry, my initial draft, and our first plan that my identified successor and I had started building out in February 2020. It was amazing how from the very beginning of planning my exit to that moment in time how consistent everything remained. Sure, things had evolved somewhat as we worked and tweaked the plans. But most of it, say 90 percent, was exactly as I/we envisioned. We built our plan electronically so we weren't dependent upon the binder. But talk about the power of proper planning.

The wave of emotion hit me in a way I didn't expect. Reviewing everything we had done to this point was fulfilling. Sometimes we get so focused on following the process we built we don't always stop and reflect on the magnitude of the event. I think all entrepreneurs have the same experiences. We are focused on executing our plans, always looking two to three years out, always grinding. But on those rare occasions that we do stop and reflect on where we are or where we have come from, it is impactful.

So I had my moment of emotion. I was going to exit "my business," "my baby." This was now more than just a thought or an exercise Larry challenged me to do. The proverbial train had left the station. Every key stakeholder, as I have outlined, was clearly aware of our plan. Many great business leaders have said, "If you want to significantly increase the odds of accomplishing something special, then share it with other key people in your life."

We shared it, and we executed the plan! Being transparent with our plan was a great component of this strategy. The transparency of our plan had now made it so there was no turning back. I took a few deep breaths, gained my composure back, and then went back to our plan. I needed to trust it, and most importantly, I realized I had a great group of people who were going to be there every step of the way with me. From my wife and family to Larry, to Kelly, Chris, Rachel, and to so many others. A special group of people who as always had my back and were all in it for it to be successfully executed.

Larry's Chapter 7 Insights

- Business continuity is not an individual sport. It takes a team to plan and execute. Bring people into the plan and trust that you can have transparency with your organization about your plans.

- We allow our egos to get in the way of business success. Remember everyone will eventually leave their business. Everyone knows it, so don't overstate your need to protect your date, plans, and times. Let your team help.

CHAPTER 8

AND THEN I FELT LIKE I WASN'T EARNING MY KEEP

One of my coaching calls with Larry Linne was an emotional moment. I told Larry I just didn't feel right handing off so much of my role to others. I had handed off sales leadership to my daughter, who was doing the job better than I did. I was starting to give roles and responsibilities to the future CEO. I was stepping out of some of the meetings because I wanted people to start looking at the future of the business versus looking to me for answers.

I am a guy who was brought up to earn my income. Work ethic was taught to me in a way that you work hard, do your job, bring a multiple of value versus what you make in income, and you make a difference at your work.

I had handed off more than 50 percent of my job and was making the same check. This just didn't feel right to me. I didn't know whether I should take those things back or add a lot of new things to offset the reduction of my role and responsibilities.

On that call with Larry, he let me express all of my feelings and logic around this concern. I told him every solution I felt was an option to earn my keep for the next couple of years.

Once again, Larry brought clarity to the situation and

gave me a huge boost of confidence. Larry said, "You have a new job. Your job is to bring one of the most difficult and financially rewarding outcomes to this business and your clients. You are being paid to make a successful transition of your role to the future. If you get that wrong, it will potentially cost the business millions of dollars. If you get it right, you could help the company grow and increase its value by millions of dollars. Going home and letting your future CEO lead a meeting, while knowing you can come in and clean up a mess if he fails, will give him a greater chance of getting it right than if you wait for him to lead those meetings when you are gone."

As usual, Larry found a way to punch me in the head and get me back on track. He was so right. I needed to be OK with focusing on the items I was still doing as a leader but allow those handoff items to be done by others, and my value was oversight, training, and a safety net.

Larry even commented, "If you only knew how much it costs companies who do this wrong! I would tell you that you should take a pay increase, or at least get a bonus if you get this to the finish line successfully. You should make *more,* not less for the job you are doing."

It reminded me that compensation at the C suite level is based on results and not hours of work.

After this lesson, I was back in gear and operating at full speed. My focus of developing the future leaders and getting the business continuity plan completely became my job. That job had purpose and value. I could see I was making a difference and was excited every day, even if I had periods of time with nothing to do. Those quiet moments meant I was having success in transition!

Larry's Chapter 8 Insights

- Our jobs as C suite executives should always be focused on our highest and best use of talent and geared toward the most critical results. When we are in the transition phase of our business, I truly believe it is where the greatest financial results occur for a business. Building the structure and people for a future of growth and making certain the foundation of the business is on solid ground is a highly valuable job.

- We usually do not need to make more money in the transition, but it is a healthy mindset to realize your value and ROI for your position is potentially very high for a successful transition. You must be mindful and think that way or you will end up getting in the way while trying to manage your ego.

CHAPTER 9

TWO SEPARATE PLANS THAT WORK TOGETHER, BUT THEY ARE DIFFERENT

The *terms financial perpetuation, business perpetuation, succession,* and *business continuity* are used frequently in business planning for the future. However, it can get very cloudy unless you define them for yourself and have clarity of what you are working on pertaining to any specific plan.

We chose to use *financial perpetuation* as the term for our ownership transition. This would include any change in ownership. This can include an internal sale to employees, family member transfers, external sale to a third party, or a merger.

We used the term *business continuity* as the term for all our people transitions and changes. Business continuity included role changes, new roles added due to growth, people replacement, and in some cases, it can be a role elimination.

This book is focused on the business continuity strategies and execution, but we reference the financial perpetuation because it will tie together through the process.

It is important to separate the two plans because it can get very cloudy for people based on their bias and priority. I have heard business owners discuss perpetuation and not have any discussions about the people side of the transition, other than taking their role.

When the business continuity plan is broken into detail, it is daunting to see the work it takes to get it right. Some of my peers who have seen our plan have cringed when they see the work behind a good plan. But it doesn't matter whether you do the plan or not; the work will still need to be done. I found it much more effective to have the plan, work the plan, modify the plan along the way, and work with clarity.

I will explain the details of our financial plan in a later chapter and explain how we reached our decisions and executed on that plan. In my opinion, the financial plan is relatively easy to develop and execute. It is the business continuity plan that is a challenge, and if not executed properly, it will have the biggest impact on the financial performance and perpetuation.

Our business continuity plan started with a spreadsheet. (See below.)

	2017	2018	2019	2020	2021	2022	2023
Revenue	XXX,XXX	XXX,XXX	XXX,XXX	XXX,XXX	XXX,XXX	XXX,XXX	XXX,XXX
Exit			Chris			Pam/Jay	Scott
Entry Position		COO	Controller	Sales Leader		CEO	
Book Trans				Pam / TBD	Pam / TBD	Pam / TBD	
				Jay / TBD	Jay / TBD	Jay / TBD	
Practice Leader out		Scott - Prof	Chris-PL		Scott - CL		
		HAM - Ind			Pam - Ben		
					Jay - Surety		
Practice Leaders	Scott - Prof	MKR- Prof	MKR - Prof	MKR - Prof	MKR - Prof	MKR - Prof	
	Pam - Ben	Pam - Ben	Pam - Ben	Pam - Ben	TBD	TBD	
	Jay - Surety	Jay - Surety	Jay - Surety	Jay - Surety	SAK - Surety	SAK - Surety	
	Chris - PL	Chris - PL	TBD	TBD	TBD	TBD	
	Scott - CL	Scott - CL	Scott - CL	Scott - CL	TBD	TBD	
	TDS - Life	TDS - Life	TDS - Life	TDS - Life	TDS - Life	TDS - Life	
	HAM - Ind	TBD	TBD	TBD	TBD	TBD	
Team Leaders		Benefits					
		P/L					
		CL					
		Admin					
Begin Training		Team Leader		Pam book	Pam book	Pam book	
		Practice Ldr	Practice Ldr	Jay book	Jay book	Jay book	
				Practice Ldr	Practice Ldr	Practice Ldr	
Begin Search		COO	Controller	Sales Leader	CEO		
			Pam Producer				
			Jay Producer				

This document was our first attempt at thinking through the future of our company pertaining to people. We included the following:

- Who would be retiring (estimated) and by when?
- Who was the replacement (if known)?
- When would we need to start searching for candidates?
- When would someone need to start training?
- What new positions do we expect to add?

As we progressed with this plan, we added more specific start dates for new hires and positions, more details on training times, and placed more potential internal candidates in spots as fillers to help us focus on their development.

It took us a few months of one-hour meetings (once a month) with Larry to get this document at a place where we felt confident we could attack it with actions and make certain it went into our annual business plan.

Once we put it in motion, we addressed it every month with Larry and our executive team to make certain we were staying on top of it. This exercise shocked me frequently in the process because of how fast and how real these transitions would take place. The hiring, onboarding, managing effective exits, training, and communication demands were a heavy lift. We had a lot of work to do, and putting it off would be costly.

If I were to do this over again, I would put more people on the team from the beginning. If we had more people working this plan, it would reduce mine and Chris's stress about getting to the finish line. We both worked hard to lead all of the transitions, and we exceeded the plan dates on most of the items. Accomplishing these dates in a shorter time doesn't just happen. The plan was the catalyst to keep us moving forward, and we filled positions sooner due to our focus and hard work.

I can't imagine I would be anywhere near retired and in this special place of my life if I had not been this purposeful with the business continuity plan.

Larry's Chapter 9 Insights

- Business continuity is one of the bigger reasons companies don't meet their financial perpetuation goals. The My Resignation Letter™ and a solid forecasted plan will motivate performance that allows for great financial rewards.

- Many plans are built in businesses, and few are followed. I highly recommend making business continuity a plan that is a recurring meeting monthly in the business. It will pay off in less frustration and financial success.

- Make certain development is happening with your people. Most employees desire continued development but they don't have time to spend in class or in programs. Look for micro learning systems. Provide time for them to learn. Spend personal time with them as supervisors.

- Another area of caution is the quality of person you choose to replace any position. It is the responsibility of leadership to continue to make the company better. I have watched business owners replace themselves with people who have the potential of becoming them. The question a business owner should ask is "what is required in this position when we are larger, more complex, and 5-10 years down the road. That may require a different person and training from the outside. You simply may not have the ability to train that person to be better than you.

CHAPTER 10

A REVIEW OF THREE EVENTS: TIME AND DETAILED PLANS WIN

I have participated in three perpetuation events at my firm. The first was a big change from the partners who hired me, with one partner remaining in the business, to two new owners who would take over all operations and structural leadership positions.

In this transition, we didn't have preparation, timelines, plans, training, coaching, or any of the key elements required to be successful. The result was exactly what someone would expect when taking a random approach. We experienced bad feelings and relationships with exiting partners and new partners who tried to figure out how to run a business while in the job.

Chris and I were blessed to have the remaining partner be someone who was trusting and allowed us to find our way. He did a great job of helping us with sales and growing the business so we could cover up some of our mistakes in running the company.

I look back and feel very lucky we survived.

The second transition, we did a little more planning. Bill was the remaining partner from the first transition and now was ready to retire. We had three people who would buy his shares of the business. We offered some basic ownership training to these new owners and brought them into executive team meetings, planning sessions, and created leadership roles for them. Basically training and developing them in leadership on the fly.

This transition went much better, but after going through this final strategy, I realize how much we just didn't know in that transition. We were reactive in training, didn't prepare the future owners for the right expectations with enough time for them to develop skills to be effective, and didn't take advantage of their potential.

We did a very good job of managing our clients and our brand in the second event. One big change was changing our name. The prior owner had his name on the door, and we realized we needed to take a new brand to the market. It was a great lesson pertaining to having a key owner's name as the company name. If a business has a desire to have long-term perpetuation of the business, it is critical to have a name that will stand the test of time.

When we changed our name at this event, we branded ourselves with a name that would last through multiple ownership changes in the future and not be tied to an individual.

In the third transfer of ownership and leadership, we had a strong plan, reviewed the plan frequently and on schedule, had a broad inclusion of all key employees in the plan, managed all stakeholders, and provided advanced training and ongoing training for key positions.

Another factor of success includes the transparency and clarity of key leaders identifying their departure date with enough time to make it happen. After the second event and my defining my exit with my resignation letter, we have made it a comfortable practice of having conversations identifying the dates they believe they will depart. As long as the date is far enough out, the exiting partner has the ability to make adjustments if they find new clarity. This entire process requires trust and open conversations among partners.

In my situation, I transitioned three roles. Each of these was over multiple years. Each had a unique plan and timelines. We were able to plan as a team for each of them. The time allowed to vet if we had internal candidates and if we needed to start to explore from outside the organization. If there was an internal candidate, were there skill sets that needed to be developed, and what was the timeline for that to position the individual for success? We always believed it was our responsibility to position the next level of leadership for success. Having the right amount of time to do it right is critical.

Setting a timeline is not only important for the new leadership but also for the exiting leader. We want the last year or two to be the most rewarding in the exiting leader's time with the company.

I also believe that having the time for the new leader to be able to work in their role while the existing leader is still at the company is another barometer of success. Having the opportunity to mentor the person in the new role can be powerful. A fine line of success in this strategy is to make certain the person leaving really is ready to go. See next chapter for clarity on preparation for leaving the business.

In another unfortunate event, the incoming partner/ leader had an untimely death. No one saw that coming. It was not only a tragic loss for his family but also for the business. The exiting partner had to recommit to lead the business beyond what he had planned on doing but had to create a new strategy. It took five-plus years for him to find and embrace the right partner. I'm glad to say in this example he and the business have been able to thrive. This is an exception, but it also suggests a backup plan should be worked into the plan as well.

The most challenging situation was when a company we knew well identified an incoming partner/leader and they failed miserably. I've seen this happen prior to the outgoing partner/leader leaving and also shortly after they were gone. In both examples, it is truly painful for all involved. Having to do it while you're still there is hard enough, but after you're gone, it can cripple a business. Having backup plans is incredibly valuable as we never know what may happen with people.

The most consistent failure is the lack of time and lack of detailed planning. Now that I have experienced a long-term plan with enough time to execute that plan, it is clearly the most important element of business continuity success.

Larry's Chapter 10 Insights

- Time is critical. Do not ever believe you have enough time to wait. The best time to plan for your exit is soon after you start.
- Backup plans are also a challenge and need to be updated quarterly as time progresses. Everyone will be happy and less stressed if this is a key ongoing strategy in a business.

CHAPTER 11

IMPORTANCE OF HELPING EXITING PARTNER GO TOWARD SOMETHING VERSUS LEAVE

Larry and I were having a conversation about a mutual friend's business challenge in 2009. We were discussing the CEO having a key producer (sales professional) who had a multimillion-dollar book of business. The producer was in his mid sixties and had given clarity that he was going to leave the business in a couple of years.

The company hired a person to replace this producer, and he began to train her. He trained her for a few months and then things started to go south. He brought numerous complaints to the executive team and felt she just wasn't good enough for the position.

After one year, they moved her off his book and let her start her own production business.

They hired a second person with a two-year plan to transition the book. After about six months, this producer had the same problems. He just wasn't good enough, didn't do all the right things, and the senior producer complained about him to management.

Management tried to insert themselves to try to make this situation work, but they ended up moving on the producer after eighteen months.

Now the firm was two and a half years into the two-year perpetuation of the senior producer with no progress. This firm hired Larry to address this situation and see if he could assist.

Larry interviewed the producer and came to an interesting conclusion. The producer knew he needed to leave, but he didn't have anything to go toward. He didn't know what he would do next and therefore was subconsciously damaging the transition.

Some of the unconscious behaviors were the following:

- Telling clients that the new person had great potential and was really learning a lot. In other words, "the person is not ready and you still need me."
- He was looking for anything that was done differently from his way of doing things and identified those items as wrong. Again, he was looking for things to identify so he didn't have to go.
- The same type of problems that occurred when he was the producer were happening with the new person. However, he was making those items look like they were only happening because of the new person.

Larry asked him, "What are you going to do when you leave?" He had no answer. He actually became very frustrated and angry when answering. He finally said, "My value is in my job. When I leave this job, I won't have value any longer."

Baby boomers have a tendency to identify themselves by what they own and what they do for a living. Therefore, when they are supposed to leave a business (even though they intellectually want to do so), they have a tendency to thwart the change because they believe they will be less valuable as a person.

In this story, Larry worked with the person to go through his tool called MyExit Plan™. It is a tool we used at our firm as well. It is three documents that include a personal focus tool that helps identify what the person will go to.

The second document is called The Knowledge Protection System™. This document allows for key knowledge to be transferred to the business. This also helps the exiting partner feel confident they have passed on the right information to the business.

The third document is the MyExit Agreement™. This document was the magic in the story above. When the producer had to write down what he would and wouldn't say to clients and what his role was in helping the producer succeed, he behaved in a way that allowed for success.

The next hire came on and the senior leader was replaced in eighteen months. It worked; he was successful.

We used these workbooks for Chris's and my departures. It took a lot of work to go through it. This wasn't because of the amount of work; it was how much thinking it took to get it right. This challenging reality shows why people can't transition. All of this work needs to be done to get in the right mindset to leave.

Chris and I went through the books, we had great success, and we are both living full lives after work.

Larry's Chapter 11 Insights

- People can't leave something; they have to go to something if they want to be committed and successful. Leaving has mental challenges and will be a fight that most people can't win. People will experience anaclitic depression when they leave something. Having something to go to will avoid this depression or dramatically decrease the impact.

- When a departing leader doesn't have a clear future, they will create distractions and cause problems to keep from leaving. Help them and the company with counseling, tools, and awareness of these issues.

- My company created a three phase system to help with exiting executives. These three systems are designed to help executives and companies get the transition right.

  o MyExit Plan™ asks the executive to work through where they are going next.

  o MyExit Aggrement™ challenges the company and the executive to think through rules of engagement as they transition.

  o Knowledge Protection System™ captures the information needed so the executive can leave and important information isn't leaving with them.

CHAPTER 12

THE DETAILS OF HOW I LET GO

Allowing your replacement to run the company while I was still there was the right thing to do. His ability to lead while I was there created capacity for me, and I struggled at times not wanting to jump into every meeting. As Larry stated, less is more. In other words, my doing less while I was there allowed the succession to have a higher chance of success.

We had created a process and a road map for success that included the specific developmental needs of our replacements. It included outside development from Larry's company, internal coaching, regular mentoring meetings, and very purposeful learning objectives. It was a good plan. But as we worked the plan, there were things I didn't anticipate.

Larry continually reminded me that *less of me* was actually more, and *more of me* was actually less. In other words, the more I was involved, the less chance they had to be successful. The less I was involved, the more successful they would become. I had to strategically insert myself when I could have coachable moments and support my replacement, Kelly, but not look over his shoulder and try to save him.

That is why it is so important that they have the ability to run the company while you're still there. This sounds much easier than it played out. I was still the CEO!

It is still my team, my company, and my baby! I found saying it was so much easier than living it.

Fortunately, I had some experience in transferring a key role in the company as I had transferred a large book of business a few years before we started the CEO transition.

I remember receiving a call from a large client during that transition. I wanted so badly to answer the clients' question and solve his problem. But I realized I had to transfer the confidence of the client to my young producer. I gave the client problem to the young producer, and he handled it perfectly. I knew if I continued to be the person who was the hero to the client, I would never transition from being the producer. It was hard, but every time I let go, it gave me and the producer more confidence.

When I look back, I realize the young producer didn't have as much experience as me, but he had skills and talents that eventually played out as being better than me. I knew this would also have to be true in my CEO transition. The company will not be better if the leader isn't better than me. So my job is to give him everything I have and allow his additional skills to allow him to be better than me.

It just so happens that the new CEO is also the producer who replaced me in that role a few years earlier. Therefore I had a lot of confidence in his skills and abilities. But it didn't matter whether he had been my prior replacement or not. He simply has skills and talents I do not have, and if I can spend the time teaching him everything I know in the job, he has to become better than me.

The sales leadership transition was much more

challenging. This is where Larry first instilled the "less is more" philosophy. He told me I couldn't be in every sales meeting.

Really? I had been running the sales team since 1998, and I had led every sales meeting for twenty-two years! The challenge was that our new sales leader was my daughter Christie.

I believed the more I was involved, the better chance she would be successful, right? My team needs me! My daughter needs me! But what a tough balance to navigate the right amount of time to be involved and getting out of the way and allow her to do the job.

Larry was helping me navigate the value of me being around when she took over my sales leader role. Frequently I would think it would be easier to just be gone and let her figure it out. But then I would see the opportunities to coach and mentor her and know it was best to have my presence, but only in the right place and time.

I would love to say I nailed this transition. Reality was more likely that she gained value by my coaching and support, but we were both learning how to make that transition successful and I failed numerous times. In my monthly coaching call with Larry, I would give him a rundown of where I inserted myself in sales and where I didn't. I was getting better every month.

She became a better sales leader than me within six months of taking the role. That gave me great confidence to continue to trust the process.

We were fortunate to have my CEO role successor be an internal candidate. We made that decision in 2019, announced it to the team, and started the future leader development process and completed the full detailed planning by the end of 2020. Announcing his new future role to the team and other key individuals in the fall had positioned us to hit the ground running with a long-term transition that started in January 2021. He could start working on his CEO brand and obtain outside executive development during that period and then be under my tutelage as CEO in training through 2021.

The first six months, we would work together with him always speaking first and I would speak second and close out the meetings. I was still the CEO, front stage. Nothing had materially changed other than people seeing me trust him with taking the lead in meetings.

June 2021 was the time to make a material change in who was leading the company.

June was our strategic planning time every year and we met with Larry and his team to design the next three-year goals and strategies for the company.

This was also a signature planning meeting as we had recently successfully completed our last ten-year plan. We were going to build out not only the next three years but also our 2030 vision. Since I was retiring in the spring of 2022, we would be planning for 2022–2025, but we needed to create a picture for our goals through 2030.

It became abundantly clear—OK, Larry had to drive this point home—that it wasn't going to be my plan! I had been a lead partner in all our planning since we started doing them in the early 2000s. But I had to accept for the very first time that I wasn't going to be here to see these plans through completion. They had to own these plans because they had to deliver on them.

Kelly, our new CEO, led the planning session, and Chris and I became participants.

This may have been the most difficult experience of my transition. Chris and I were disappointed in how the session played out. It wasn't as sharp and disciplined as our past sessions. The new CEO wasn't holding people accountable, and Chris and I were not being utilized effectively. It seemed like a disaster!

I struggled to write that last paragraph because the reality was that this session must have been the hardest thing a new CEO could do. He had to run a planning session that was his and his future partner's, who was taking over for Chris (CFO), first major event. I look back now and realize that he did a great job. Yes, I had to coach him on some items after the meeting, and he took that coaching very well and made adjustments. He and the CFO partnered up at and after the session with excellent leadership.

What I thought was a terrible session was actually the exact session it needed to be. It was uncomfortable having Chris and me looking over their shoulders, and they were not perfect. The lack of perfection was my issue and not theirs. The expectation should have been that they would not be perfect and Chris and I were there to help them at the meeting and after. I failed them in that I was there to judge them on their performance.

What a great lesson to learn! This would allow me to evolve my expectations and coaching/mentoring over the next eleven months until I departed.

After building these plans in June, it was very clear that all things for 2022 and beyond wouldn't be *my* plans.

I became a passive participant in the 2022 tactical goals and planning.

I want to be clear. I was still the CEO and was responsible for the performance of the company so I had to be aware of what was going on and ultimately either make or approve the decisions we were making. My CEO successor would meet with me in advance of meetings and major decisions and gain my perspective. He would also meet with me afterward and we would debrief on the progress and how things went in those meetings.

This rhythm of communication allowed him to move from backstage CEO to front stage performer. In July 2021, we shifted to having me go first in leading meetings, and then he took over and ran them to completion.

Our team was looking at him for leadership and guidance and everyone saw me as purely a mentor.

Two additional things happened during this bridge phase. I identified it as such as it was time that the transition was taking place in real time. One was guilt I started to feel and the other was the capacity or time I found available to me that was new and different.

My role shifted in the final five months to be responsible for capturing the intellectual property and systems to memorialize key components of our past that established the foundation for the future. I spent a large portion of my time identifying critical intellectual property and core principles that would need to stay in place after I left. These were items I would verbally communicate or execute on a regular basis that would leave the day I was gone.

I had fun building out some tools and videos that

carved these items in stone for the organization to keep into perpetuity.

Letting go was a hard thing to do. However, if you have time, you have a great chance of evolving the pieces that need to be let go. I was fortunate to have a great team and partners who helped me navigate the mistakes and good decisions through the process.

Larry's Chapter 12 Insights

- Leaving a business you own, you lead, you created, you built is incredibly difficult. Knowing that and starting the journey by accepting it will be hard.

- Ego *is* the enemy of an effective exit. If you can't set your ego aside, you should leave without staying to mentor and coach the next person. It will be difficult for them to go alone, but better than fighting against your ego.

- If you can set your ego aside, get a coach. It is similar to coaching your kids. You can't see things clearly. So get a coach who can give you clarity as you go through the process. Make sure they will tell you the truth, even if it is tough. You don't have to agree with everything they say, but you should listen. Also, make sure they understand the personalities and culture of the firm so they can give good advice.

CHAPTER 13

DEVELOPMENTAL PLANS

It is so important to invest in the talent you are bringing into the future. Learning the job is certainly important, but so many additional factors are critical and are typically ignored.

One area frequently ignored is how to be a responsible owner. As I look at businesses with multiple business owners, I frequently see people who act entitled or selfish as owners. These types of owners cause problems and can destroy the culture of a business.

We believe future owners need to understand the responsibility of creating value for the company, be a leader, help others be successful, know how to be a critical thinker, be aligned in culture, solve conflict with other partners, act cohesively, and continue to perform at a high level.

These things don't just happen! It requires training and development. We can't assume someone will just "get it."

It is also important to evaluate the gaps of current skills versus desired skills of the person and the job they are entering. Taking the time to evaluate skills in depth allows for a more detailed plan of development. With our two senior leaders, Kelly and Rachel, we put them through an extensive program that began with a full week of assessing their knowledge and skills as executives.

From that evaluation, they went through a three-year development program to master those skills.

Another key point Larry made clear to us in this process was what skills we were developing. Many business leaders think their job is to teach them what they know so they can be their equal when they take over. We were a business operating just over $10 million in revenue at the time we began our business continuity. Our growth was accelerating in the final years. Larry opened my eyes when he said, "You don't need to find someone that can do what you do. You need to find someone who can run a business two to three times larger than your business today."

He walked me through the differences of how larger business CEOs and CFOs have a different role and require different skills. This was one of the reasons we felt it necessary to have us mentor and coach but make certain they were receiving outside coaching as well. They needed to have skills we didn't have today.

We also challenged our next-generation executives to engage with each other with their development. This would allow additional learning and create teamwork and a partnership.

Chris and I had worked so close together as we led the business for twenty-two years that we knew it would be powerful for the next leaders to have the same level of trust and partnership moving forward.

I also found it necessary to step back from my way of doing things and allow the next generation to do things differently. I would pause when I saw something different and ask myself, "Is this the wrong way because it isn't how

I would do it? Or is this a different way to get the same or better outcome?" I would think long and hard before ever correcting something. In many cases, I found that the new technique, method, strategy was going to be better than what I did.

Again, this became another spot of checking my ego and letting others find their way.

A good developmental plan with time to execute will also allow you to see if you have the right person in the right seat. This can be very valuable and is usually very evident early in the process. If you don't give yourself enough time, you won't be able to find the right person.

Finally, it is critical to have frequent check-ins with those you are developing. Don't simply send them to class and hope they learn. Chris and I met with our future leaders frequently and purposefully. We would ask them to teach us what they were learning so we could mentor and coach them.

Spending time with them and giving purposeful coaching will give them a great chance of success.

I can't stress enough how important it is to develop your future talent. If you don't invest in this development, you will have a high probability of failure and that means you stay a lot longer than you should.

Larry's Chapter 13 Insights

- As Scott mentioned, I was blessed to go through an elite developmental program (BEI Exit Planning Institute). I have learned the power of information to knowledge to wisdom and eventually to simplification. The training I received has been passed on to hundreds of people and I get to see their success from that training.
- Be purposeful in training.
- Check in frequently and use the technique of asking the trainee to teach you what they learn and to ask for your advice.

CHAPTER 14

SAYING GOODBYE

I truly never expected to write this chapter. I had committed to Larry to have the first draft done prior to my officially turning over leadership of the company. But due to COVID, I lost a week of productivity in writing this and had to push several business events and projects back.

The retirement celebration events took on a life of their own. Three weeks of "last" times together events were overwhelming. The organization put on an amazing final retirement event that was such a blessing and very humbling. My last celebration event with our top performing producers from the previous year was another event that meant the world to me due to my career having so much involvement and passion for sales and our salespeople.

My last leadership in-person meeting with the two new leaders, Kelly and Rachel, was so amazing. I was able to see these two great leaders who were ready to take this company to a place of continued greatness. It was truly a blessing. To experience each of these special groups of people was tremendously impactful.

Then there was the last team meeting. We have our team meetings every Monday at 8:00 a.m. We were still in a virtual environment, more to do with our remodeling of our office building than COVID at this time. I had once again traveled to my place in Florida. I had asked Kelly and Rachel, since that Monday would effectively be my last official day as CEO, if I could join the meeting and say goodbye to the team. As always, they agreed and totally supported my evolvement. The way our meeting was structured, the CEO always wrapped up the meeting. Kelly and I had been sharing this responsibility for the better part of a year now. The first six months, he went first and I wrapped it up. The last six months, I went first and he wrapped up. This meeting, he suggested he go first and I wrap it up.

When I met with the entire organization on the final day, I had my notes in front of me outlining the message. Having hundreds of team meetings a better part of twenty-five years now, it was second nature to stand in front of them all and speak. Well, not today! My voice immediately choked up as I started to talk. Next were a few waves of emotion as I looked at the faces of the people in the room that I loved so much.

I quickly shared my well wishes to the team, thanked them for thirty-four phenomenal years, and then abruptly said goodbye and signed off the Zoom meeting. It was not how I expected to end the session, but it was the only option due to my emotions.

I was on my patio at my condo, the same place eleven months earlier where I had my first emotional moment. This moment was more intense and had such finality to it but was combined with more joy than pain. I had finally executed my exit plan. The one that started four years earlier. The plan that I truly enjoyed working through with Kelly and our team. The one that Larry had begun with a challenge to me and had been there each step of the way with and for me. If I'm truly honest, I might have cussed him under my breath a few times along the way for bringing this all upon me! But it was done and I realized I had accomplished something very special.

My wife was with me at the condo during this last session with the team. She was in another room when I had my moment. But she knew something was not quite right with me. I shared with her my emotional experience. As usual, she was very supportive. But a few minutes later, she said, "Let's go run some errands." It was time to move on and upward to the next phase of our lives. A phase I am very excited about because I know exactly what I want to do and where I want to spend my time. A phase that holds a bigger future. My exit from my business was complete. But my plan for the next phase of my life had already begun!

Larry's Chapter 14 Insights

- Saying goodbye will be difficult no matter how you play out your exit. But it will be much harder if you do it poorly. I have watched executives make terrible exit decisions, and it is solely because they didn't do the hard work to plan and develop talent. So they justify their poor work by either selling the business off to someone who won't care about the people or just dump the business and let the team figure it out but blame them for the failure.

- Saying goodbye is a part of the process. Remember everyone will eventually leave the business. Every option will be challenging. But the best option is when you do it your way and build something great. It will be OK to be sad and happy and emotional in that moment.

CHAPTER 15

GET A COACH

I speak frequently about Larry Linne in this book and that not only says a lot about Larry but, more important to the story, is how critical it is to have a coach or a guide.

I can't imagine how much I could have screwed this up without having someone to help me through all of this. I believe it is important to know what value can be brought from a good consultant or guide in this process. Let me outline the valuable components of what Larry did for me. Hopefully it will provide others with a checklist of what they may need.

Honest feedback – On many occasions, I would find myself just needing to talk through things with Larry. He would listen. After I was finished, Larry would give me feedback on what he thought pertaining to all I would say. At times, he would confirm my thoughts and give me support to help me keep going. At other times, he would kindly give me a new direction for my thoughts. I believe this is where he helped me stay mindful and eliminate my biases toward how I was seeing the world. Of course, we also had the moments where Larry would figuratively punch me in the mouth. In those moments, he recognized it was time for a tough message that I needed to hear. These messages would be delivered with compassion and love, but they were direct and very honest.

Clarity of plans – He helped me make certain my

plans were complete and clear. I struggled at times to get complete clarity of what was needed and how to get things done. Larry helped organize my plans and sharpen what I needed to do. I can usually think of all the items needed in a plan, but Larry helped organize those thoughts in a way that helped me be highly productive.

Modification of plans – We both saw the need to modify our plans as we progressed through the execution. We had different times where we would see the need to change course and make changes. I found it valuable to have another set of eyes on these plans. My partner (Chris) and I would go over the plans with Larry on a regular basis and just make sure we were on the right path.

Provide training to the future leaders – We were fortunate that Larry's company, InCite Performance Group, has in-depth training for future leaders. Larry had been through a high-performance executive training program early in his career. He has a passion for executive development, and his team has incredible experience and skill to deliver elite training. Our team was blessed to have this resource and we worked with his entire team to get all the knowledge and wisdom possible. Kelly and Rachel continue to work with Larry's team after the transition.

Allowing the balance of emotion and logic to execution – I mention numerous times in the book how emotions stepped into the picture for me. I found it very valuable to be able to share that with Larry and even become emotional with him during calls. Larry has that good German stature and doesn't allow emotion to get in his way very often (I am sure he gets counsel for that as well), but he was kind to allow me to get emotional when needed and to balance it with logic and mindfulness and use all of it to get results. I never felt the need to apologize to Larry for my actions or words as I processed through this. He allowed me to be me.

Being a friend – Larry is also in the later years of his career, as noted by his resignation letter. Many times he would just ask questions about me, my family, and even my feelings. He was available by text, phone, Zoom, or in person if I needed it. I felt like I was his only client at times, and that was because he was incredibly invested in my and our company's success.

Played the room like a fiddle – I learned later that he was masterful at knowing when to communicate with others in the organization to keep the train on the rails. He reached out to the future CEO a few times to give him clarity of what I was going through and make sure he understood how to make the process go smoothly. He spoke to Chris on occasion as well to make sure the entire system was working. He knew where I needed help and would work with others where necessary but never violated trust or confidence in the process.

Believing in the process and the people – He was very aware of the talents of Chris as my partner. He was also very aware of all of the key players, including my daughter Kelly and Rachel. He knew our sales team and the details of how our company was built. He helped me navigate the talent development and trust in our people due to his being an outside voice of confidence.

Taught me – Larry taught me so much through the process. I can't imagine getting through all of this without having the knowledge and wisdom shared by him. He understood the psychology of what we would be dealing with through the process, the steps we needed to pursue, and all the points of navigation along the way.

Humility – Larry also was able to see where he was wrong or where he was learning something new. We both recognized that every situation is different in a perpetuation story because every organization has different people, processes, history, geography, clients, and performance. That meant he didn't know everything and he recognized that from the beginning. He frequently expressed we were creating something that has never been done before versus following a strict model.

Larry's Chapter 15 Insights

- I am humbled by these thoughts. However, I see perpetuation failures daily in my business consulting. People don't get it right and having someone to talk to is critical. The outline of items above is certainly valuable.

- I would add the need to have someone who has experience with all aspects of business continuity as well as behavioral science experience to the list. People are the key to success and understanding the predictability of humans is very valuable in a perpetuation experience.

- Business Enterprise Institute (BEI) is a firm that teaches and certifies exit planners. I received my CExP™ through BEI and I would highly recommend finding someone to help with the organization and execution of a complete exit plan. The ROI in getting it right is worth the investment in someone who will guide a business owner through the mental challenges and the complex issues that must be navigated.

CHAPTER 16

HOW YOU KNOW YOU WERE SUCCESSFUL

The bottom line here is to leave the business better than you found it and have a foundation for the next generation to build something even greater.

As I grew and matured as a leader, I understood that being a servant leader was a pretty special way to lead. Please know that I had moments in time when I drank the Kool-Aid of people telling me I was talented and thought I was bigger than the business. Looking back at that time, I didn't like myself for that behavior.

Over time I learned to understand the role of a leader. Ultimately, I think the answer lies behind the question "Did we leave the business better than we found it?" Actually we can say this about so many other parts of our life as well—our family, our community, etc.

We are only stewards of our time during the time we lead our businesses. I relate my role as a leader as somewhat of a "business Sherpa." We guide our team through both challenging and clear paths to ultimately accomplish the summit that we desire to reach.

But my ego can and still does get in the way. As I was thinking about what I might want to selfishly hear my team say after I am gone, I would want to hear, "Scott would have never done it like this." A statement like that may pump my ego, but it would mean I didn't transition the business to others who are confident in their abilities.

But true success is defined when the team actually says, "Why didn't Scott ever think of this?"

I would suggest success is leaving the business better than you found it and where you hired, mentored, and coached your successors to be building something even greater than you were able to build. Turn it over to a new Sherpa who knows the terrain toward the next mountain greater than you do. Your job is done. Be proud and be thankful.

I know Chris and I are very proud of what we have built, and that includes the talent who are already making the company greater than we could have thought possible.

Larry's Chapter 16 Insights

- Leadership is hard. It truly takes a selfless person to lead an organization into proper transition. You must set your ego aside and guarantee the world sees the next generation greater than you.
- Measuring financial performance, employee engagement, and client satisfaction will allow you to see if the business is truly greater than you had built. If you do the right things, those results will be evident.

CHAPTER 17

BUILD YOUR LEGACY

As mentioned early in the book, Larry challenged me in the beginning of this journey to follow the Barry Sanders model. I needed to leave before my prime. Clearly I am no Barry Sanders, but the goal was to leave while I still had gas in the tank and some runway left. I believe I accomplished this to a large degree, but ultimately time will define this as it does for each of us.

I realize now that every perpetuation and business continuity event in our company has a legacy tied to it, as there will be in yours as well. Looking at our company history, the 1998 event left a multi decade career and family legacy tarnished by greed. All parties left empty and without any love for each other. I believe I spoke with the former managing partner only one time after the transaction, and that was truly by accident. As I stated earlier, he dictated all terms of the deal and then left angry. This was certainly not a legacy I wanted to define me. Yet I have witnessed this type of departure far too often. People work for decades, lead their businesses to a special place, and then leave on bad terms and leave the business with a poor chance of success.

In each of the others, we all worked in alignment of each other's goals and wishes and most importantly with the best interest of the team and the business. I can tell you this was still a lot of hard work, but the positions of the team and business along with the goodwill associated with each was refreshing.

What will your legacy be? Is it already defined? Are you retired in place, still getting paid for the job you did five years ago? Are you crawling toward the finish line? Does the team wish and look forward to the time you're not there? Are you afraid of naming your successors or helping the next generation have hope due to clarity of when they can lead? Are you positioning the business and team for a bigger future, or is it more about you and your ego? Will someone find you dead at your desk? These are examples of the legacy you may create without a plan or purpose.

It is also important to realize our departure will have an impact on our family and numerous other stakeholders. Give them the gift of a purposeful exit from your business, and make sure the legacy you leave behind with each of them is one you can be proud to own.

We have choices on how we go about this journey.

I know my journey and those of my most recent partners were full of emotions, but those emotions were a wonderful part of the process. We have choices to make. What will you be? Your plan will ultimately define your legacy.

Thank you, Barry Sanders, for setting the example!

Larry's Chapter 17 Insights

- It is your legacy. Do you want to have it told to you by chance, or do you want to control the narrative? I believe the script can be written and performed if you desire to do the work!
- Know that Scott White did pull off the perfect Barry Sanders act. He was clearly one of the top CEOs in the independent insurance agency business. People came to him from all over the country to get advice as he built one of the fastest growing and industry leading agencies in the small town of Marquette, Michigan. I am proud to have worked with Scott, and I would encourage everyone to follow his footsteps and become the next Barry Sanders.

CHAPTER 18

WHAT OUR NEXTGEN SAYS ABOUT THIS JOURNEY

We have a team of next-generation leaders who are running the business now and are doing an amazing job. I thought it would be valuable for you to hear some comments from them about how this transition has impacted them.

Kelly

My true feeling is a feeling of thankfulness. I am grateful because the purposeful nature of the transition has allowed each stakeholder to either be in a position to succeed or in a position of minimal disruption.

The Future Leaders Program brought tremendous energy and excitement!

As an observation, it was interesting to see how the end of one career could still provide a defined future path for the organization and teammates that is bigger than the past.

The resignation letter created a sense of urgency. It made it real for me, for us. Personally, we knew that it could create opportunities for us individually to have a greater leadership role. This created hope and excitement for the future. A future we could have our fingerprints all over.

The process allowed us to accept the responsibility of leadership. As we accepted the responsibility, we recognized that titles no longer matter. Buy-in to leadership meant being humble and serving versus being the boss. I saw a different role than I had perceived, and that came from working side by side with Scott. The tone was set by Mr. White.

You can't do this alone! Get outside coaching!

There is never enough time. You always want more!

Christie

The fact that they took time to plan it out continued to show their investment in the agency and their careful consideration of the VAST culture when making such a large decision.

I got so much energy in the fact that they trusted me and saw this potential in me that there was no way I wouldn't dedicate 100 percent to this position. I was *comfortable(ish)* taking this leap because I knew they would support me and help provide tools, resources, and mentoring to help me.

We knew the day would come when he would retire, but the letter coming much earlier than his actual retirement date was scary. However, it proved the carefulness and thoughtfulness he put into this decision. He didn't hide behind anything, including his emotions, and it allowed us to start thinking of the transition period in a completely different way. When we knew how much time we had before his retirement, we were able to break down the time we had left into periods where we could have someone identified/hired by and allowed time for a lot of shadowing and training, which was priceless.

Rachel

I feel the way they approached the transition set me up for success. I had both of their support, which helped greatly in earning the team' s support. Additionally, we overlapped for a period of time so I was able to slowly assess what the current responsibilities were and how I could absorb and put my own mark on them.

This opportunity allows me to have more flexibility and control while still offering learning and growing opportunities.

It (resignation letter) was very beneficial to learn of his plan and help understand how that role was going to be filled and by who. My day to day is greatly impacted by my partner in the CEO role, and I was happy to be aware of what was happening both with his exit and the onboarding of the new CEO. It helped me focus on my role, moving it in the direction that I wanted to, and that matched the new CEO's direction.

Tom

I feel energized, confident, and empowered.
Scott instilled in me from day 1 to leave it in a better

place than you found it, and I believe they accomplished that. Kelly and Rachel want to do the same.

As a leadership advisory group, we all had skin in the game to live, breathe, and improve on the foundation Chris and Scott provided us.

Today I am in the best headspace I've ever been in. I share this not to talk about me but to provide context on the impact Scott had on my career, and with Kelly taking over as leader, both of them being there pushing me, moving my cheese, and all done because they both cared is something I will never forget. Energy created and gratefulness I feel since that day are driving me to continue the legacy that was built and do my part to leave it in a better place than I found it.

Heather

He would often make comments like "I wish I was still in my forties to see where this thing goes next" and "The next decade holds so much more promise for this organization than the past decade did." He was very quick to point out that the people coming behind him had much more capability and aptitude than he ever did. This type of confidence in our current leadership team is what has given me and the rest of the agency a lot of hope for the future. He always enabled us to do/be our very best and often believed in us *way* more than we believed in ourselves. Scott has always and will always be one of my greatest mentors.

Larry's Chapter 18 Insights

- This group of leaders was trusting and very positive through the process. They owned the commitment of becoming the best future leaders they could become. It is a partnership to develop future leadership, and the future leaders have to put in effort to be successful. This group did a great job of three years' worth of leadership development.

- It is encouraging to see the energy in the words of these future leaders. The process did what was needed to make the My Resignation Letter™ effective.

APPENDIX

THE FINANCIAL PERPETUATION STORY

This book is about business continuity as a part of the overall perpetuation of a business. I felt it necessary to share the financial portion of our perpetuation decision as well. It may fill some gaps in understanding what we accomplished.

Here is our story:

At some point, everyone will leave their business. Larry shared with me how he worked with prospects in his exit planning coaching. He said the first question he asks is "Are you going to leave your business?" He would talk about how funny it was to watch most people ponder the answer.

Of course, the answer is yes. Everyone will eventually leave. However, he found it interesting that people would ponder the answer because they had never really thought about it, at least at a level where they had to do something about it.

I realized when he asked me that question that I was certainly going to leave at some point. It became obvious to me if I leave on my terms, in my time frame, and *have control* of all the factors involved. It will be a greater experience than if any of those items were not in my control.

Larry and I discussed the ways people can leave a business. They can sell to a third party, sell to internal personnel, sell or gift to family, die, become disabled, or become insolvent or file for bankruptcy. I had to think about every option and where I could experience the greatest joy and financial reward.

Doing nothing and just dying in my office chair certainly didn't seem very attractive. I was going to miss a lot of joy with grandkids, seeing things of life in slower motion, time with my wife, and more.

I also found that waiting until very late and not properly preparing the business and myself was not going to allow me to protect my desired outcomes. I was not willing to leave my future at a level of chance when I didn't have any idea where my health would be at that time.

I concluded that I needed to perpetuate thoughtfully and with a multiple-year strategy.

As stated earlier, being purposeful is a valuable concept in perpetuation and business continuity. I wanted to be purposeful about financial perpetuation as I knew it would align with our business continuity.

Spending time with business partners thinking through goals and strategy for success creates incredible clarity and shows how often a business must change directions to stay on the best course for success.

This concept showed very true in one planning session down in Florida. Everything we had been working toward and our core perpetuation strategy was kicked in the teeth in a single session. The revelation was that we were not going to be able to perpetuate internally. We were very emotional about this change because we had spent dozens of years fighting for that possibility.

However, through the planning session, we realized it wasn't a moral issue or right or wrong to perpetuate in this manner. We realized we could continue to meet individual, corporate, client, and all stakeholder needs through an external perpetuation strategy and remain in control of our business.

New models of private equity and capital partners were being introduced, and we felt it truly changed the game. We were able to easily accept that our desire for independence as a business could be redefined as having control of the business and personnel decisions in our company. These new options were incredibly attractive. We could insert unheard of capital into our business, have control, and increase our performance due to new resources and tools.

It was January 2015. Our leadership and partnership team (one and the same at this time) had gathered for our annual planning event. Larry joined our planning session as he had done for the past eight years.

He had provided us with pre-work for each of us to come prepared for another successful session. This year we were in Tampa, Florida, leaving the cold winter of the Upper Peninsula of Michigan. Getting off-site, away from the routines of both work and family, always gave us a heightened level of focus and an opportunity to build our relationships together in ways we didn't get throughout the normal year.

As always, one of our key discussion topics and annual strategic initiatives was perpetuation or business continuity. Larry always brought something to every planning session that would make us feel uncomfortable.

This year he asked each of us to share our personal exit strategies and challenged us to specifically include the year we anticipated retiring.

We also reviewed our buy/sell agreement where it was specific that in the calendar year you turned age sixty-five you were required to sell back to the company. An owner could, if all agreed, continue to work past sixty-five, just not as a shareholder. The goal was always to keep stock transitioning to current minority shareholders and new and younger future partners. We didn't want someone to be in their seventies and eighties controlling the stock of the company when they may have already "retired in place." Even more valuable was the need to make sure new owners were given the opportunity to buy in and keep a balance of shares through multiple generations.

As Larry took us through our business continuity discussion, things started to shift in the room. One of the majority partners was four to five years away from sixty-five. We needed to start to build out her exit strategy. The initial plan was to possibly have the three minority partners who were part of a 2011 perpetuation event look to increase their shares in the company along with identifying three younger talented associates to gain a minority shareholder position. It was evident that I would still be about five years from age sixty-five, and the chances of completing her exit were predictable and guaranteed financially to succeed. As we looked out toward my exit, due to the large amount of my ownership, it became less guaranteed that we were positioned for that event to be successful.

During our session, we were notified that one of our

good friends in the industry had announced they had sold their business. The fact that the three principals were very young—two in mid-thirties and one in early fifties—caught us off guard and introduced another possibility for us to potentially consider as a financial perpetuation strategy.

Up to this point, our sole focus had always been to internally perpetuate our business. In fact, we were viewed as a business that had completed a very successful event in 2011 by transitioning a senior level owner to three new shareholders. We were featured in *Michigan Agent Magazine, Rough Notes Magazine, Independent Agent Magazine,* and within our consulting group as an agency/business that had not only had done well in 2011 but our plan to stay internal was viewed as a "Best Practice."

As we continued to plan in Tampa, we worked through what it would take to perpetuate me and Chris as the two majority shareholders over the next eight years.

The three current minority partners weren't sure if they wanted to buy more stock into the company when 2023 would arrive because two of the three would be in their later fifties to early sixties. The other shareholder who could buy shares would be in his late forties. They wouldn't have enough years to buy more stock and then quickly turn and start selling at age sixty-five.

Larry took us through an exercise that opened our eyes very wide and frankly changed how we viewed our ability to continue to internally perpetuate. In our business, it is typically our sales team (producers) that has the financial wherewithal to buy into the company. These producers control most of our key customer base, making them logically very important to have as shareholders.

Larry's math lesson in 2015 showed us that by 2023, it would take a minimum of three new shareholders to perpetuate one majority shareholder. So with the current minority shareholders not looking to purchase more stock in 2023, we would need to ultimately hire, train, and make successful producers to our team who could potentially purchase more stock. We also needed to identify timelines to purchase the next group of shareholders a few years later. Looking out now to 2023, it seemed more likely it would take five producers to perpetuate one majority shareholder. We had two majority shareholders leaving at that time!

In our traditional business model, if you hired five producers, you would be successful if two of them succeeded—with three being considered great. It also was typically for every three producers one of them may want to become a shareholder and/or be considered as a candidate for partnership. Therefore, to have five future owners, we would potentially need to hire fifty-plus producers in the next two to three years! This was close to impossible because we would not have enough candidates in our marketplace, didn't have the ability to afford this many new hires along with the necessary support staff, and the turmoil that would be created for our team would be overwhelming.

So once again, our planning session had created a major mind shift on how to successfully internally perpetuate in 2019, 2023, and soon again in 2026. During this seven-year period, we would be required to transition at least 77 percent of our current shareholders. We needed a different strategy and plan.

Time is critical to plan and execute a successful financial transition. We didn't give ourselves enough time. This is why this book is about business continuity success and not our financial perpetuation success. We did an amazing job with what we had to do, but I can assure you that we should have started the financial perpetuation the day we first purchased the business to remain 100 percent independent and 100 percent in control.

When you think you have enough time, you'll be surprised that you could have used more. Circumstances will change over time, and adjustments will need to be made. This is hard, purposeful work to get it right.

I started this chapter by introducing that an entrepreneur can sell to a third party, sell internally to family or key employees, go bankrupt, transfer due to death or disability, merge with another company, or simply walk away. All of these options have financial and emotional consequences.

I considered the consequences of all these options and quickly came to my decision that maintaining a model that allowed future wealth creation for individuals and local control were the two options that had to happen. The reality hit me that these options were not a given outcome by just showing up. Hope was certainly not a good strategy. We were not going to be able to execute a traditional internal sale.

To remain a model that allowed for future internal people to have wealth creation and maintain local control, we would have to either sell internally or find a capital partner that would allow that control. This new clarity of our desired outcome also gave us a gut check that we had a long process in front of us to maximize the potential outcome.

We had to have the right earnings to justify the desired financial outcomes needed to justify the transfer, establish clarity of role transition including the timing, and a tremendous amount of work in managing communications. This plan had to be established and executed. This began eight years prior to the final action being completed!

We were blessed to find a partner who was committed to our staying in control. Acrisure was our partner of choice, and we have experienced numerous years post sale with incredible results. Acrisure has exceeded our expectations!

All goals have been met for all stakeholders.

They provided the cash to manage the transition of large shareholders and provided a future model where the next generation could be owners. We were provided great wealth creation today and in the future as well as control of the business in almost every area. As long as we performed, which we always did, we had complete control of the business.

However, let me be clear. Do not wait! Today is the first day to get started on your exit!

Larry's Resignation Letter

Letter of Resignation for Larry G. Linne
Submitted 7/20/2018

Date 7/20/2025

Partners at InCite Performance Group:

This letter is my official resignation as CEO/President at InCite Performance Group.

After 20 years at the firm, I believe it is time for me to step down and allow the next generation to run the company.

We have accomplished the right things in developing the business continuity, client experience and value proposition, brand in the market, and financial performance to allow me to make this move.

I will proudly tell the marketplace about the incredible talent and brighter future of this firm with your leadership. I consider it an honor to be part of a firm that developed the future talent to be greater than my abilities. Your ability to run this business without my leadership is a compliment to me and to all of you.

My availability in the future will be 100% up to you, your leadership team, and our clients. I want to respect the leadership of this firm and not require them to ever tell me it is time to go. This resignation is my way of telling you "I think it is time for me to go". I want you to know that I mean it! If you decide you want or need my skill or talent as part of your future strategic objectives, I will consider the offers. This allows you to have no pressure to ask. It is also no pressure for you to worry about my ego. And, it allows me no pressure to say yes to stay on.

I have spent 62 years working on my intellect, skills, financial results, and talents. "If" I decide to continue to work outside of InCite PG, I am certain I can find healthy opportunities. Of course, it would never be in competition with InCite Performance Group. I respect you and all we have built too much to ever try to damage what we have created.

So, do not worry about my ego. Do not worry what I am thinking if I am out and you never ask me to do anything again. Right or wrong, I will simply assume it is because we did an amazing job of business continuity. The best strategy may be to get me as far away from the business as possible for a while!

However, your asking me to do any work in the future would also be an honor (if it is a fit for both of us). I pray that the ask is based more on want than need. A "want" would be something that is a win for both of us. A need would possibly mean that we didn't do what we needed to do to get us fully perpetuated.

I am thankful and feel very blessed at all we have accomplished. This is the best consulting firm in the world. It is because of hard work, teamwork, innovation, creativity, and amazing talent!

Thank you,

Larry G. Linne
DATE 7/20/2025

Each year after writing this letter, Larry has worked with his team to identify specifics of his job that need to be learned or developed by the next generation of leaders. They own the responsibilities of this development and are making this letter an evolving reality.

Larry writes an updated letter every year to identify

the new realities that exist for the company. He has to do that because the company continues to exceed the goals placed in the original letter. The energy created and focused on by the team has made the business more fun and exciting every year.

Scott's Resignation Letter

Resignation letter

Effective (9/4-/21), (11/1/21), (12/31/21), (5/30/22) I am tendering my resignation as CEO of Acrisure LLC, dba VAST. Since August 8, 1988 I have been privileged to have worked in this agency. The people I have been blessed to have worked with over the years, and currently, truly are the one's who make this decision to be bittersweet. I cannot convey how special my career here has been. Our very "noble profession" of helping people re-build their lives is one I have been proud to be a small part of.

Though I have been working towards this day, having transitioned my roles as advisor, sales leader and now CEO still makes this difficult to announce. But as I reflect back since we became an Acrisure partner in February 2016 I am extremely proud of what we have accomplished together. Having expanded throughout 100% of our building, revamping our physical plant to meet the current and future needs of our team and clients. Successful transitions of the City and UP 44N teams and clients. In addition bringing Rachel on to our team as COO, helping Chris and Vince transition from their leadership positions, introducing new Sales Leadership, (), and (), as CEO is extremely rewarding.

I have always said that we are only stewards of our time while we are here. It is both necessary to leave the agency in a better place than when we joined it but more importantly to position it for a "Bigger future". I can clearly say as I write this today that the team including the new leadership is ready to take this agency to places that I could of only dreamed of. I am excited to watch from a far as the future unfolds for the VAST team. Please know my heart will always be here.

Thank you and God Bless

Sincerely

Scott M White

SCOTT WHITE, CIC
ceo/cro/partner/risk advisor
VAST
300 South Front Street, Marquette, MI 49855

Assessment to Begin the Journey of Your Exit

Below is an assessment on determining where you are in the process and a path to creating your exit.

When do you expect to leave your business?

Do you expect to work the same as today until your exit?

Have you identified your successor(s)?

Do they know who they are?

Are they on your team?

Would you want to have a future role after giving up your leadership role (sales, mentor, projects, other)?

What are the goals you want to accomplish before you exit?

What legacy do you want to leave

- your family?
- your team?
- your community?

If you have a plan, what have you communicated to the following stakeholders:

- your family?
- your leadership team?
- your team?
- other stakeholders, key clients, and/or centers of influence?
- others?

Have you written or prepared your My Resignation Letter™? Who have you shared it with?

Do you have clear plans toward your future after working in the company?

When assessing prior leadership transitions, what did you like or dislike about those events? What do you want to do differently?

What have you done to assure your business is positioned for future success?

ACKNOWLEDGMENTS

Resign to Success is the story of my business succession journey. It encapsulates my thirty-four-year journey in my business as an independent insurance agent. Having been a party to multiple business succession events in my business during this time, along with witnessing numerous others over the years, there are way too many people to recognize for influencing me throughout my career. That being said, I will share those who have been intimately involved in my journey.

My team at VAST. These are the most talented people in our industry. Without their support over so many years, this book would never have been necessary or possible. They always had my back during the tough times but also were there celebrating with me during so many wonderful times. My partners Pam, Tom, and Jay helped me see that the traditional way wasn't always the right way and it was OK to pivot and explore new avenues.

To Greg Williams, the CEO of Acrisure, who I was introduced to in October 2015. I can't thank you enough for your amazing leadership. Partnering with you and Acrisure in 2016 was the best business decision I ever was a part of. I also thank his team, especially Andy Schutt and Sozon Vatikiotis, for all they did for me personally and the VAST team.

Rachel Johnson and Kelly Reed were both instrumental in making this journey so special. The two of them made the final months of my transition so very special. Rachel as our new COO is as talented as anybody

I have ever worked with. Kelly as my successor CEO is more qualified than I ever was to lead our company. Working firsthand with him for the last two years was something I will always cherish. The leadership at VAST is in awesome hands.

My two longtime business partners and great friends, Bill Hetrick and Chris VanAbel, have been there from the very first day of my business journey on August 8, 1988. Bill, who hired me, was my coach, mentor, and made sure that I was always positioned for success from day 1. He invited me into partnership with him and Chris. He showed us all how to do business succession the right way in 2011. He exemplified "servant leadership" more than any person I have ever known. Chris, who was with me every step of the way through December 2021, was the most multi talented person I ever have worked with. There wasn't one phase of our business that she didn't totally understand. In her fifty-two years at our business, she started as a part-time file clerk and culminated her career as one of the most talented and respected COOs and CFO's in our industry. Most importantly, she always had our people number one; her caring and leading them was instrumental in our success. She always told me things whether I wanted to hear them or not. Always making sure we did things "the right way." Their partnership and friendship I will forever treasure.

I met Larry Linne, my coauthor and special friend, about fifteen years ago. From our very first call as our business consultant, Larry challenged me to be a better version of myself. Not only as a leader and business owner but as a husband and father as well. He has been there with me through many challenges and celebrations. He helped me to grow as a young CEO who "drank the Kool-Aid" and needed to understand the definition of servant leadership. I can best describe Larry as a phenomenal version of a Swiss Army knife. He possesses unbelievable skills, both business and personal, that I am always amazed at and most importantly has proven himself in his results over time. Many times I have relied on him for advice and counsel, and he has always been there looking out for me, my family, and my team. This book would never have been possible without his challenging me to do this the right way, to build a plan, share it, and execute it. He believed this story was worth sharing and has spent countless hours working on it to bring it to life. Thank you, brother. LUM!

I wish I could say I didn't miss an event of my girls, Carrie and Christie, while they were growing up, but unfortunately I did. I traveled a lot during my career, and my wife, Jill, and the girls were always supportive of me no matter what.

My oldest daughter and her husband, Corey, have given me my two most precious gifts in the world: my grandson, Jack, and granddaughter, Elizabeth. I am so proud of their marriage and beautiful family and the talented professionals they have become.

My youngest daughter, Christie, who has succeeded me as sales leader at VAST, continues to amaze me. Her first two years in the role, she crushed my best years leading our sales team. I am tremendously proud of her growth both personally and professionally. I am so thankful she will continue to be a part of the VAST leadership team for years to come. I can't wait to see what she does next.

Jill has been with me for over forty years now. She never wavered back in 1998 when I said I wanted to change from a very stable banking profession to a career in sales. In fact, being a young personal insurance sales person was quite a leap of faith for us both. She has always been my rock and my strength. Today we are very blessed with the family and life that we have. But none of it is possible without her love and support. She is my best friend and the love of my life. I am extremely excited to share this next phase of my life with her. Truly because of her, I know that *Resigned to Success* will be very special!

Also, a special thank you to BEI for the incredible foundation of knowledge and process.

Printed in the United States
by Baker & Taylor Publisher Services